Helping Children
with Feelings

Helping Children
Pursue their Hopes
and Dreams

T0383630

A Guidebook

Helping Children
with Feelings

Helping Children
Pursue their Hopes
and Dreams

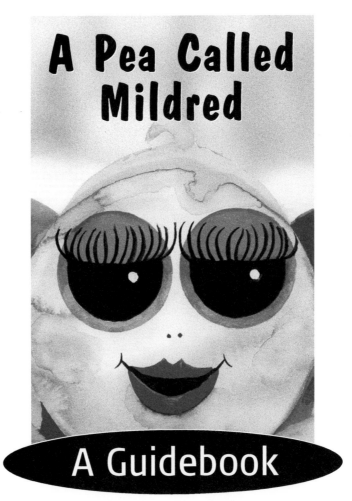

A Pea Called
Mildred

A Guidebook

Margot Sunderland

Illustrated by

Nicky Armstrong

Routledge
Taylor & Francis Group

LONDON AND NEW YORK

Note on the Text
For the sake of clarity alone, throughout the text the child has been referred to as 'he' and the parent as 'she'.

Unless otherwise stated, for clarity alone, where 'mummy', 'mother' or 'mother figure' is used, this refers to either parent or other primary caretaker.

Confidentiality
Where appropriate, full permission has been granted by adults, or children and their parents, to use clinical material. Other illustrations comprise synthesised and disguised examples to ensure anonymity.

First published 2000 by Speechmark Publishing Ltd.

Published 2017 by Routledge
2 Park Square, Milton Park, Abingdon, Oxon OX14 4RN
711 Third Avenue, New York, NY 10017, USA

Routledge is an imprint of the Taylor & Francis Group, an informa business

British Library Cataloguing in Publication Data
Sunderland, Margot
    A Pea Called Mildred : helping children to pursue their hopes and dreams
    Guidebook – (Stories for Troubled Children)
    1. Storytelling – Therapeutic use 2. Child psychology 3. Learning, Psychology of
    I. Title II. Armstrong, Nicky
    615.8'516

ISBN 9780863884559 (pbk)

Contents

ABOUT THE AUTHOR

MARGOT SUNDERLAND is Founding Director of the Centre for Child Mental Health, London. She is also Head of the Children and Young People Section of The United Kingdom Association for Therapeutic Counselling. In addition, she formed the research project, 'Helping Where it Hurts' which offers free therapy and counselling to troubled children in several primary schools in North London. She is a registered Integrative Arts Psychotherapist and registered Child Therapeutic Counsellor, Supervisor and Trainer.

Margot is also Principal of The Institute for Arts in Therapy and Education – a fully accredited Higher Education College running a Diploma course in Child Therapy and Masters Degree courses in Arts Psychotherapy and Arts in Education and Therapy.

Margot is a published poet and author of two non-fiction books – one on *Dance* (Routledge Theatre Arts, New York and J Garnet Miller, England) and the other called *Draw on Your Emotions* (Speechmark Publishing, Milton Keynes and Erickson, Italy).

ABOUT THE ILLUSTRATOR

NICKY ARMSTRONG holds an MA from The Slade School of Fine Art and a BA Hons in Theatre Design from the University of Central England. She is currently teacher of trompe l'œil at The Hampstead School of Decorative Arts, London. She has achieved major commissions nationally and internationally in mural work and fine art.

ACKNOWLEDGEMENTS

A special acknowledgement to Mattan Lederman who, at age seven, drew an entire set of pictures for all of the five stories in the pack. Several of his ideas and designs were then adopted by the illustrator.

I would like to thank Katherine Pierpont, Charlotte Emmett and Ruth Bonner for all their superb skill and rigour in the editing process, and for making the long writing journey such a pleasurable one.

I would also like to thank all the children, trainees and supervisees with whom I have worked, whose poetry, images and courage have greatly enriched both my work and my life.

ABOUT THIS GUIDEBOOK

If a child is going to benefit from the full therapeutic potential of *A Pea Called Mildred*, this accompanying guidebook will be a vital resource. We strongly advise that you read it before reading the story itself to the child. By doing so, you will come to the child from a far more informed position, and so you will be able to offer him a far richer, and more empathic, response.

This guidebook details the common psychological origins and most relevant psychotherapeutic theories for the problems and issues addressed in the story. If you read it before reading the story to the child, it will prevent your coming to the child from an ignorant or closed viewpoint about why he is troubled. For example, 'I'm sure that Johnny's school work has gone downhill because he is missing his Daddy, who moved out a few months ago' may be an accurate or inaccurate hypothesis. There may be many other reasons for Johnny's problems in his school work, which have not been considered. The problem may well be complex, as so many psychological problems are. Coming from a closed or too narrow viewpoint all too often means that the helping adult is in danger of projecting on to the child *their own* feelings and views about the world.

Very few parents are consciously cruel. When something goes wrong in the parenting of a child, it is often to do with the parent *not knowing* about some vital aspect of child psychology or child development, or a lack in the way the parent was brought up themselves. There is still a tragic gap between what is known about effective parenting in child psychology, psychotherapy and scientific research, and how much of this is communicated to parents via parenting books or through television and the press. So this guidebook is not about blaming parents. Rather, the aim is to support. More generally, the aim is to heighten the awareness of *anyone* looking after children about how things can go wrong (usually despite the best intentions), and about how to help them go right in the first place, or to get mended if they do go wrong.

This guidebook includes what children themselves have said about what it is like trying to cope with the problems and issues addressed in the story, and describes the stories they have enacted through their play. It includes a section that offers suggestions and ideas for things to say and do after you have read *A Pea Called Mildred* to the child. The suggestions and ideas are specifically designed to help a child to think about, express and further digest his feelings about the particular problems and issues addressed in the story. Some of the exercises are also designed to inspire children to speak more about what they are feeling through *their own* spontaneous story-making.

Everyday language is not the natural language for children to use to speak about what they feel. But, with an adult they trust, they can usually show or enact, draw or play out their feelings very well indeed. Therefore many of the exercises offered in this guidebook will support the child in creative, imaginative and playful ways of expressing himself. Also, so that you avoid asking too many questions, interrogating the child about his feeling life (to which children do not respond at all well), some of the exercises simply require the child to tick a box, 'show me', or pick a word or an image from a selection.

INTRODUCTION

What the story is about

Mildred is a pea with dreams. She has great plans for her pea life. People tell Mildred that her dreams are pointless, as she is just another ordinary pea. But she is not prepared to be just another ordinary pea. So, although it means going into a very lonely place for a time, and letting go of everything she knows, Mildred does not abandon her dreams. Eventually, with the help of kind people along the way, Mildred ends up doing exactly what she has always dreamed of doing.

The main psychological messages in this story

✳ When you encounter all sorts of adversity, do not abandon your dreams. Just put more energy into them.

✳ Do not put up with unfulfilled potential – go and fulfil it!

✳ When the present feels tight, narrow or pretty hopeless, dreams of beyond-the-now can expand everything.

✳ You have to have the dreams in the first place for them to become a reality.

✳ Every idea comes out of a dream.

✳ If the people around you are offering only pessimism and discouragement in the face of your hopes and dreams, find people who will offer you optimism and encouragement.

✳ When you put time and energy into making things happen for you, life can open its doors to bright new worlds. If you just let things happen to you, this can bring the drudgery of sameness, or even a living death.

✳ Dreams formed in childhood do not need to be escapist fantasy; rather, in later life, they can become something intensely real and deeply lived.

Who the story is for

The story is written for all the following children:

* Children who have been given too little encouragement to follow their hopes and their dreams.

* Children who are too despondent or defeated to go after their hopes or their dreams.

* Children who just cannot be bothered.

* Children who have lost their will to fight for what they want.

* Children who are too busy surviving, so hopes and dreams are a luxury they cannot afford.

* Children who think that hopes and dreams are just for other people.

* Children who do not follow their dreams because they are too afraid of failing.

* Children who want to want something, but because they do not know what they feel, they do not know what they want.

* Children who are floating down *somebody else's* river, following *somebody else's* star.

* Children who only dream small dreams for themselves, from a fear of being big.

WHY CHILDREN NEED HELP WITH THEIR HOPES AND THEIR DREAMS

The average school curriculum allocates very little time to the important subject of dreaming and hoping – the importance of not abandoning your deepest wishes and so not abandoning yourself. Yet a major contributory factor to a fulfilling life is the ability to dream dreams for yourself.

The ability to go after a dream, from its seed as an idea in your mind to its fruition in the world, is very important. The ability to imagine 'other worlds', in whatever form they take, gives life both richness and colour. Rather than simply living with what is in front of you and automatically going with whatever comes next, the ability to dream and to imagine brings horizons of possibility – a view to 'a place beyond-the-now'. So when the present feels tight, narrow or pretty bleak, dreams can expand everything. Moreover, when the going gets tough, dreams provide hope and bring a real sense of something 'around the corner'. This said, many adults are often very poor at dreaming for themselves. Many put far more effort into planning Christmas or a summer holiday than into planning their lives!

If children get into a way of being in the world which means just drifting along and having no important thoughts, such as 'When I grow up I want to . . .', then, as an adult, they may similarly just drift into situations, jobs and relationships that really do not suit them at all, as revealed, for example, in such remarks as 'I just drifted into marriage with her', 'I drifted into debt and gambling', or 'I just drift along, day by day, in my dead-end job.' On the other hand, if children are helped to have a dream for their lives, and with what to do once they have had such a dream, many can then be enabled to live with far more interest in and anticipation about the future.

What a child takes from a therapeutic story or an encouraging parent, teacher or therapist can have a marked effect on his inner world, and have a real effect on his imagination, and his sense of his own potential. Indeed, seeds sown in a child's inner world may not become fully flourishing plants, metaphorically speaking, until the child has left home, but such early 'sowing' can have a profound effect in later life. In short, education of the imagination is as important as education of cognition, and yet the former is often given too little credence. This is why therapeutic stories such as *A Pea Called Mildred* are a must.

Doubters may ask, 'But what is the point of spending time in a dream world in your head, if you have to go back into a reality which is pretty bleak, such as a parent hitting you?' Such sceptics forget that every child has an inner world as well as an outer world. What happens in their inner world has a considerable effect on their outer world. It is the child's inner world that gives emotional meaning to their outer world events, for it is in the child's inner world that a sense of hope can be either fuelled or blighted that the capacity to go on in the face of adversity can be strengthened or squashed. It is in the inner world, that a feeling of 'I will' or 'I'll show 'em!' is given power or not. It is in the inner world where heroes are thought about and identified with; where moments of warmth, encouragement and appreciation from a teacher or kind relative are treasured, repeatedly replayed and used as nourishment.

For children from very troubled backgrounds, dreaming dreams for their lives can be *especially* important, providing or sustaining a sense of hope in their inner world, when in their outer world they may feel unbearably impotent or hopeless for much of the time. Dreaming dreams means that they can have in their heads a very different world from the world of their painful outer life. This different world is not just a world to escape to, but a world to go to for creating, building or laying foundation stones, which, in later life, can be brought into reality.

WHAT LIFE IS LIKE FOR CHILDREN WHO HAVE MET WITH TOO LITTLE ENCOURAGEMENT FOR THEIR HOPES AND THEIR DREAMS

> We may choose to grow, to stagnate, or to decline, and in a world where there is little encouragement to grow, most of us may not do it very much or at all. (Rowan, 1986, p13)

Many children and adults harbour a private dream, but that is exactly how it remains – private. Too often, dreams remain 'only dreams', when in fact they carry great potential. Too many children and adults simply lack the courage or belief in themselves to move themselves through from dream to dream-come-true. It is all too common to see the tragedy of a life that never quite bears fruit, because there has never been 'quite enough dream', or never quite enough energy and will behind the dream. In many cases this is because the person has met with too little encouragement in their life.

In *A Pea Called Mildred*, Mildred meets with only discouragement from her father. This is true for too many children, whose dreams are not taken seriously or are actively discouraged, or whose imaginings are shamed or ridiculed in some way.

Nat, aged seven

Teacher to Nat (looking at Nat's picture of a submarine): 'Wow, Nat, that's great!!'

Nat: 'No, it's not. My Daddy says I'm stupid. Am I stupid?'

(By the end of the school year, with this warm and encouraging teacher, Nat did believe in himself, and stopped believing the critical father in his head.)

Nat to his teacher: 'Hey, look at my super spaceship! See how strong its engines are. It's the sort of spaceship that can take me anywhere.'

You can see how easily, without the right person to encourage them, children like Nat may just give up their hopes and dreams and develop a belief system categorised by 'What's the point?'; 'Why bother?'; 'It'll only come to nothing, it always does'; 'I'm useless'; and/or 'I can never get anything right'. In other words, a child's too-low motivation to get on with things, his inability to carry things through to the end, his sense of flatness, apathy or lack of interest, his very low self-esteem or his move into antisocial behaviour may stem from too little encouragement and sometimes active discouragement for his ideas, his hopes and his dreams.

> If a little girl wants to fly we do not just say 'Children don't fly'. Instead of that we pick her up and carry her around above our heads and put her on top of the cupboard, so that she feels to have flown like a bird to her nest. (Winnicott, 1949)

Understanding why some children abandon their hopes and dreams, or never really have any in the first place

Children who are too defeated to go after their hopes and dreams

> Bright Star, would I were as steadfast as thou art. (Keats)

A child who has suffered from too many traumatic disappointments or active discouragements can all too easily give up his hopes and dreams (if he ever really had any in the first place). His sense of goodness about the world can then become too frail, and he can give up hope of ever finding a better world (which of course is what dreaming is all about). Yet another child who suffers from too much pain and hurt *does not* lose sight of his dreams. Why is this?

If a childhood includes a very solid and deeply loving connection to someone, then that child can suffer awful setbacks, traumas or discouragements without plummeting into the depths of defeat and staying there. There will still be some light, hope and sense of goodness in his inner world – all essential ingredients for the capacity to dream. Indeed, the emotional fuel that carries an idea of a dream from its seed to its eventual fruition often comes from some loving connection. A loving connection can sustain a child through the most difficult times. Without one, life can be one big struggle. Whether this connection is to a parent, a nanny, a teacher or someone totally unexpected, it gives the child a sense that 'I have something of value to offer, I am potent.'

A child who never experienced a loving connection, or whose loving connection has been cruelly broken, may have his creative endeavours in life blocked; or they may not take off at all. Such children can be plagued in life by self-sabotage, self-doubt and self-hate. Defeated children who do not have these strong foundations in love often do not reach out for praise or encouragement. Some do not get angry either. There is hope and life in anger. Anger is a protest, as opposed to a giving up.

A defeated child is like a wounded soldier who has lost his will to fight. He is too weak to get up and go after what he wants. Hence the lifelessness of depression, which is all too prevalent in many children as well as adults. Depression leaves no room for dreams.

But what can defeat a child so? Here are some common causes:

⁕ The child has experienced too many interactions of dominance, criticism, belittling, shaming or put-down.

⁕ The child has felt unable to light up a centrally important person in his life, and/or he found too little light in this important person which could have lit *him* up.

⁕ The child could not get Mummy or Daddy to be proud of him, *however hard he tried.*

⁕ In babyhood, he lost too much hope and faith in his capacity to make an impact. His crying did not bring his Mummy or brought her to him too late. The baby whose cries are repeatedly unanswered eventually stops crying. This is often thought to be good, but it is actually a matter of defeat.

⁕ There has been something too weak, or too troubled, in the child's connection with one or both of his parents in early childhood.

⁕ The child has experienced too many adults' needs or demands for him to be a certain way.

⁕ The spark in the child was never fully lit, because the adults in his life were too frightened of their *own* life-force, excitement and passion to be able to encourage those in their child.

✳ A deeply loving connection has been traumatically broken because a most important person in the child's life has left or died. This is only a problem as regards the fuelling of dreams if either the break happened before the child had time to really take in the love, strength and goodness from that relationship and make it his own, or the child has no loving others in his life.

If a child has suffered from too much defeat in any of the ways described above, then there will be no point in saying to him 'Brighten up!'; 'Can't you find something better to do than just watch television all the time?' or 'Just find something that interests you – a hobby, a cause – or join a club'. The goading optimist is missing the point. Yalom, an existential psychotherapist, says, 'To create something new, something that rings with novelty or beauty or harmony is a powerful antidote to a sense of meaninglessness' (Yalom, 1980, p435). This, again, is missing the point for children defeated too early by life. They often do not have enough 'pzazz' in them to want to create anything. School work; creating a song; a picture; a fabulous fish; a story – all can feel pointless. Sometimes there is a sense that whatever they create will be worthless or dead, just as they may have felt that their love was a worthless or a dead thing for their parent. Many deeply defeated children have lost all faith in their potency – in being able to affect anything or anyone.

Even if he does get started, the too defeated child may then get bored half-way through. John, aged eight, got interested in things to start with, but then, after about 15 minutes, his energy always waned and he would stare out of the window. In counselling, he made up a story about a car whose battery was too low 'so it never gets me up the hills I want to go up'. John's mother was very depressed. He felt he could never light her up.

A note is necessary here on how a few defeated children can, at some point in their lives, rise like a phoenix from the ashes into a life position of 'I'll show 'em!' Writing in 1926, Freud called this defence 'reaction formation' (see Freud, 1979). A few children who have felt unbearably defeated and impotent at some point in their lives (often very unexpectedly), do shift into a completely different life position. Over time, they have made a powerful *unconscious* choice to defend themselves against their intolerable feeling of defeat and move into potency, success and even fame. For some, it is a case of 'I couldn't make Mummy love me, so I will make the world love me instead'. Marilyn Monroe is a classic example of this, as are some other famous film stars, artists and atheletes. One can only marvel at the incredible drive of such children. Yet, tragically, for many, their defeat which they are defending themselves against so strongly will live on to haunt them, to sabotage and undermine their happiness in some major way. In adulthood, some recognise that this is happening and so seek professional help.

Children who do not go after their hopes and dreams because they have lost the will to fight for what they want

It is not only contemplation that is important, it's only when the contemplation bears fruit in action. In the act of doing I will discover who I am. (Descartes)

If hopes and dreams are backed by too weak a will, there may be too little emotional fuel to push beyond the initial inspiration to embark on the action needed to turn the dream into a real possibility. Wishing without will does not get you anywhere. Endless wishing without willing eventually enters the realm of musing or escapist fantasy; whereas, as soon as action fuelled by will follows wishing, it is no longer escapism.

Tragically, some children are plagued by feelings of 'can't be bothered'; 'don't care'; lethargy and boredom, because their will is too weak. They are often wrongly referred to as 'lazy children', when in fact they are too shamed or discouraged by life. Laziness in children by and large points, not to sloth, but to some kind of trauma, oppression and damaged will.

What can cause such damage to a child's will? At around the age of two (the 'terrible twos'), and again at adolescence, there are vital developmental stages in terms of the development of will and the capacity to protest. There are various reasons why these developmental stages can go wrong, resulting in the child having a weak will in later life.

At these natural stages of protest, sometimes a child is too frightened of his parent to engage in a battle of wills; or the parent is so afraid of losing her authority that she asserts her dominance in ways that frighten the child into submission. Sometimes at home (or at school) the child is too often shamed. The parent can give the (usually non-verbal) message that she will only love, approve or be proud of the child if he is compliant. Some parents are so threatened by a child's wilful behaviour and separate self that they can accept nothing less than total compliance. Some actually say, 'I needed to break his will.' Parents or other family members (such as older siblings) may assert *their* will in loud, dramatic or frightening ways. As a result, the child establishes a way of being in the world which is all about navigating someone else's feelings rather than asserting his own.

Children who want to want something but, because they do not know what they feel, do not know what they want

These are children whose spontaneous feelings, impulses and explorations of the world have at some time been too controlled by someone else. In other words, some children who cannot want or dream for themselves have felt intruded on by the adults in their lives with over-controlling behaviour, or with emotionally or physically smothering attention. They have not been given enough emotional and/or physical space to respond, explore, act, feel, or love, in the way *they* want to.

Some children who do not know what they feel, and so cannot dream for themselves, have had a parent who was grossly out of tune with them: a parent who, for example, would pick them up suddenly when they were sitting very contentedly; who would cuddle them just as they were engrossed in a toy; or who would leave them on the floor when they were screaming to be picked up. Similarly, some parents think they are being helpful by giving constant 'educating' attention when a child is playing with his toys, while they may in fact be suffocating the child's spontaneous responses.

> If every time B is spontaneously playful the mother or father takes over the play and embellishes it with their own play, the child will come to experience an extraction of that element of himself: his capacity to play . . . The parent has taken away the meaning of the toy. (Daws, 1997, p180)

The danger of such unaware intrusion is that the child can lose all sense of what *he* wants, and grows up knowing only what the other person wants, or wants him to want. The following are typical examples of parental intrusion on a child's spontaneous expressions:

✳ 'Hey look at this (not that)!'
✳ 'No, put the building-block like this, not like that . . . '
✳ 'No, look, this bit goes on that bit, don't put it there.'
✳ 'No you don't want that, you want this.'
✳ 'Play with this now . . . '
✳ 'No, you don't feel that, you feel this.'
✳ 'You're just tired.'
✳ 'Don't do that, no don't do that. No don't do that either . . . '
✳ 'You're being far too slow, dear, let me finish it for you.'

As a result of being controlled in this way, the child can lose all joy in his own sense of 'I can . . . ', 'Look, see how I can . . . ', 'Look what I did'. Furthermore, any supposedly playful interaction between adult and child becomes a dismal failure of 'co-creation'. If this happens repeatedly over time, the child can lose (or not form in the first place) his enthusiastic engagement with life. Instead, his energies are taken up with fending off intrusions – anticipated or actual.

Later, as Mrs F changed Ben, he caught sight of his foot and started trying to get it into his mouth. He seemed to be enjoying this, when she took hold of his foot and playfully pushed it into his mouth quite firmly. Ben whined and stopped playing with it. After a while he caught sight of his pram and reached his arm out to get hold of the side, which he tried to chew. Mrs F thought he might be wanting to get back into it, so she sat him up in it. He worked his way down on to his back and seemed content lying in the blankets and trying to get hold of one to chew. Then she tried to get him interested in a toy and he soon became discontented. Increasingly Ben gave the impression that he was making himself into a 'thing' as much as possible when he felt intruded on. He had the look of someone who is holding on, wondering what's going to happen next. (Glucksman, 1987, p347)

Children who cannot dream because they are floating down somebody else's river, following somebody else's star

> Career moves and personal moves like marriage had been instigated by someone else – Mother, Nick – and I had merely persuaded myself to go along with them and called that my personal decision. (Thrail, 1994, p186)

Some children can be very clear about their parents' dreams for them, but have no idea about their own dreams. This is often because they have never been encouraged to have a separate thinking/feeling self with *their own* ideas, initiatives and dreams.

Very early on in life an idea can get planted in a child's mind that he would like to be, say, a doctor. Sometimes it is a family tradition that is going unquestioned. Sometimes his parents are living their own unfulfilled dreams through their child. Whatever the cause, the idea is planted so successfully that the child comes to believe that it is his dream. The opinions of a mother, teacher or other major influence can all too easily become inner voices in a child's mind which then accompany him through life on a daily basis, directing him in the 'right way to go'. Often, children fall into a reverential attitude towards their parents or teachers who say they know what is best for them. Sadly, many children lose their *own* dreams like this, or never make them in the first place.

Many of these children, at some point, lose their momentum and interest because they are 'floating down somebody else's river' and following somebody else's plans for their life. To begin with, in order to get the approval of his parent, the child may put enormous energy into following his parent's star, and then, after a while, wonder why he feels so empty or unexcited by his school work. It may only be years later, when he drops out of medical school (or its equivalent), that he realises it was never *his* dream.

If children with such a history can be helped to find what they really want, a spring of real energy and motivation can surge within them. Without therapeutic input, however, many children with this sort of background never find out what their own dreams are, and some, tragically, reach old age never having lived the life they wanted to live.

Children who are too busy surviving, so dreams are a luxury they cannot afford

Some children are full of so much fear, anxiety, grief or anger that no one has helped them to work through, that they are not emotionally free enough to go into a world of positive imaginings. They simply do not have the psychic space in their minds. They are too busy just surviving. If, for example, a child sees Daddy beat up Mummy, the world can feel so bad that the child loses faith in there being any good in the world – at least any good that will endure over time. And a child has to have enough hope in the goodness of the world to go after a dream.

There are also children who have felt too much emotional pain, and so have cut themselves off from their feeling lives and live in their heads. Although this is a safe retreat from suffering more pain or hurt, the price is often a lack of real excitement about anything. Such children can appear dull or deadened. Other children who have felt too much emotional pain just move into the realm of destructive fantasy (about, for example, who they want to beat up tomorrow), rather than creative fantasy and dreaming, and hoping for something really good in their lives.

Children who have made an unconscious decision to be ordinary

Whether on a conscious or an unconscious level, some children feel that going after dreams is not for them, it is only for other people. These children can then 'find themselves' not bothering at school, sometimes not caring about their appearance, or just not really caring, full stop. Somewhere along the way they have made an unconscious decision to be ordinary, to have what Eric Berne calls a 'banal life script' (cited in Stewart & Jones, 1987, p107).

Some children try to stay unnoticed, because they have been so shamed in their life so they keep anticipating further shaming in response to how they are, what they do or what they say. One ten-year-old boy who had been repeatedly shamed, both at home and at school, explained that he was 'just doing life by hiding in the undergrowth', and, if he got to the end of his life without really being seen, then he would be very pleased.

Some children have squashed their strengths and abilities, even made themselves plain and dull, so as to leave the 'stage' free for someone else in their family to be exceptional, extraordinary or beautiful. In other words, they have stifled their own life-force in some way, so as not to threaten or upstage a parent or sibling. This is often done totally out of conscious awareness. They may have developed a belief that 'There's not space for both of us to be successful around here', or that 'Because you are so clever, I seem so stupid in comparison.' Or they may have picked up from a dominant family member a sense of 'Don't you dare threaten me', or 'I'm the clever [or beautiful] one round here, so back off'. (These perceptions may be based on reality or just imagined – projected on to the successful sibling or parent.) Sometimes, the reason is a fear of arousing envy or jealousy in someone in their family.

Whatever the reason, these are children who play out, all too realistically, the life of a Cinderella who never goes to the ball. For some, it takes time in counselling or therapy to unleash them from their 'banal life script' – their marriage to being ordinary. For others, the unleashing can happen through a teacher or other adult truly believing in them.

Children who do not follow their dreams because they are too afraid of failure

Sometimes a child has no dreams for himself, or does not go after them if he has, because it just feels too dangerous. The danger is that he might fail or be criticised, ridiculed or shamed. So it is far safer and far less anxiety-provoking to just drift along, going nowhere in particular, than to actively follow a dream or goal. Such a child may only observe the dreams-come-true of other children; he may watch films about them or read books about them.

> Like many children who do not create dreams of their own, he metabolised and enjoyed other people's fantasies, fantasies that gave a narrative structure to his own longings, as they were encoded in the books he chose to read. (Person, 1996, p22)

WHAT YOU CAN DO AFTER YOU HAVE READ *A PEA CALLED MILDRED* TO THE CHILD

This section offers ideas for things to say and do after you have read this story to the child. The tasks, games and exercises are designed specifically to help a child to think about, express and further digest his feelings about the story's theme.

As previously discussed, children often cannot speak clearly and fully in everyday language about what they are feeling, but they can show or enact, draw or play out their feelings. Therefore, many of the exercises in this section offer support for creative, imaginative and playful means of expression. They are also designed to inspire a child to respond further by telling his own stories.

In order that you avoid asking the child too many questions (children can soon feel interrogated), some exercises just require a tick in a box, or the choosing of a word or image from a selection.

Please note The tasks, games and exercises are not designed to be worked through in chronological order. Also, there are far too many to attempt them all in one go – the child would feel bombarded. So just pick the ones you think would be right for the child you are working with, taking into account his age, and how open he is to the subject matter. Instructions to the child are in tinted boxes.

✳ Where are your dreams?

Have you:
Run out of dreams? ☐
Never really had any in the first place? ☐
Stopped putting any real imagining time into dreaming dreams for yourself and for your life? ☐
If you have lost your dreams, how could you get them back, as Mildred did? Write or draw how below.

There is often so little (if any) space on the school curriculum for children to really spend time dreaming their dreams of how they want to be or what they want to do, and then imagining being it or doing it. So getting children to spend time with their dreams, or thinking up new dreams for themselves, is important. Some children may have dreams, hopes and wishes, but all too privately, all too quietly, never voicing them or ever letting themselves really know them. Furthermore, just thinking about dreams is often too dry, whereas taking the time to fully imagine a dream – to flesh it out in an art form – can mean that it is vividly experienced. This next picturing exercise, is designed to help children to envision, or rather, to dream while awake.

✳ Draw your wishes or dreams as Mildred did

- ◎ Draw your dreams as Mildred did.
- ◎ Now draw a picture of what happens when someone gives you three wishes which come true.
- ◎ What do you feel when you see your wishes and dreams in your drawings?
- ◎ How can you keep them safe in your mind, so you don't give them up?
- ◎ Who might spoil them? And if they do, or if they try to, what could you do then?
- ◎ Who can help you with your dreams and your wishes?
- ◎ If you can't have your dreams and wishes come true just the way you dreamt them, what might you have instead? For many people a version of their dreams or wishes can come true, but not in the same form as they first dreamt them.

✳ Visiting a magical place

Visit a magical place in your imagination. Now draw it.
Who would you invite there? What would you do there?

✳ The journey to your dream

Children can be helped to keep on the journey of their dream if they know what to expect on a typical dream journey. Here are some of the stages of a typical journey towards a dream and things you might on the way. Copy the illustration in Figure 1 to give to the child.

The first step towards a dream coming true is to dream it in the first place!

Sow the seeds of the dream in your mind. This means imagining your dream as if it had come true. What are you feeling? What are you doing? Where are you and who are you with in your dream-come-true?

Difficult things you might meet on the way towards your dream coming true include obstacles, discouragement, spiky people, people or problems that feel like brick walls, and feelings of aloneness, as if you are in a wilderness. (Don't give up here. It's where some people give up, because they lose sight of what might be around the corner.)

Good things you might meet on the way include kind people, people who encourage you, people who help you with your dream, people who really understand how much you want your dream to come true.

Now fill in the picture called 'The Journey to your Dream'.

If you are already started on your journey towards your dream, these are things you may well meet on the way. They are things that most people meet at some time on the journey to their dream come true. If you have met any of these already, colour them in.

Figure 1 The journey to your dream

✳ Two common dream stages

Look at the pictures called 'Common Stages on a Dream Journey'. They are about two stages you often meet on a journey towards a dream coming true. We have drawn these stages so that, if you meet them, you will remember about them.

The good nothing-much-happening stage
This stage is all about allowing your mind some rest time from your dream. Research has shown that the most successful people in the world are not those who work all the time, but those who work and play. It is often in the play time that the best ideas come for the work time. Play brings a space in your mind, so ideas often pop up unexpectedly, because there is room for them to pop up. If you work and work without any time to drift, play, or 'slob around', your mind has no chance to cook up exciting new thoughts and ideas.

The empty nothing-much-happening stage
This stage is empty rather than fertile, because it does not bring any exciting new thoughts or ideas. It is just an empty nothing, rather than a creative nothing. It has a heavy feeling about it.

Note You can explain to a child how a field that lies fallow for a season will bring forth rich new crops. It is like that with your mind. Nietzsche (1993, p11) said, 'All good things have something lazy about them, and lie like cows in the meadow.'

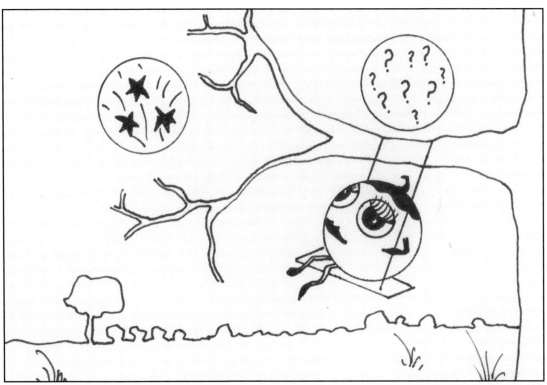

This stage is good because although there can seem to be no change in your outer world yet, things are happening very actively in your mind, eg, planning, ideas, new creative thoughts.

The nothing-much-happening stage is empty rather than good and creative, because it does not lead anywhere. It is just an empty nothing rather than a creative space. It has a heavy feeling about it. You may get into this stage, if you have lost the magic feel of your dream, or someone has squashed it.

Figure 2
Common stages on a dream journey

✳ **A quick-fire way into the dream**

Finish these sentences or draw your answer very quickly so that any spoiling or critical voices in your mind have no time to come in.

I wish I could _____

_____

One day I'd like to _____

_____

What I want to do when I grow up is _____

_____

What I really want to be is _____

_____

What I wish for me and my life is _____

So what I'm going to do in my life now towards making my wishes come true is

_____

_____

_____

_____

_____

_____

✳ **All about hope**

What do you want to do with your life, before you die?

_____

_____

What would you like to be remembered for?

_____

_____

What are your hopes? If you have no hopes, did you have some once? If you did, how did they get lost, or die?

_____

_____

Have you ever had a hope or a wish about something that someone squashed or trod on in some way? If you did, draw what it felt like to have it and then to lose it like this.

✳ Travelling in time

Make a picture of your life at the moment, and then a picture of your wished-for-life, now or when you grow up. Now put your drawings next to each other and choose a miniature toy to be you. Place the toy on your 'life at the moment picture', then move the toy as you speak, make up a story of how you get to the 'wished-for-life picture'.

Start your story 'Once upon a time . . .'

✳ Helpful things to tell children about following their dreams

Feel the fear and do it anyway. (Jeffers, 1987)

If you don't let yourself dream, nothing will happen.

Whatever we create in our lives, whether it is an omelette, a multinational corporation, or a love affair, begins as an image in our minds. (Glouberman, 1989, p2)

There is no failure, except in giving up.

Dream wild dreams – and only then pare them down if you have to.

Rather than the whole dream, a part of a dream can come true, or it can come true in a different way from the way you dreamt it. Keep your eyes open to this happening.

I've learned that, if you wait until all conditions are perfect before you act, you'll never act. (Brown, 1991, p104)

Nietzsche (1993, p23) said, 'To lie still and think little is the cheapest medicine for diseases of the soul.' The value of dream time like this can be enormous.

Don't give up having dreams for your life, just because the first one or two didn't come true, or because you didn't wait to see if they would come true.

You could spend a lifetime reading the menu of what is on offer in this life on Earth (and it is an endless menu), and find by the end of your life that you were so busy deciding, that you have never actually gone after anything.

If dreams are based just on 'shoulds' – 'I should do that', or 'I should get to be cleverer than my brother' – they often end up as fizzled-out dreams because they are about 'oughts', not about real wishes. With adults, many books and business ideas never get finished or carried through, because people are not very, very excited by them.

Using the arts is an excellent way of helping children to explore and put flesh on the bones of their dreams. Making images of a dream (in art, a poem or in sandplay), is far more powerful than just talking about it. It is like planting the seed of the dream in the richest soil, letting it incubate there, and tending its growth. Rehearsal of the dream through the vividly imagined activity of an art form is spending time and energy empowering a dream.

Through artistic expression, such as painting, clay or poetry, a child can actively imagine himself into a different place, and make discoveries of new emotional landscapes. Through the performing arts, a child can enact new ways of being in the world, and try out different roles – for example dancing or playing in music a stronger, more assertive self or a more gentle, centred self, so as to experience a transportation into richer ways of being. In fact the mind cannot distinguish between vividly enacted experience and the real thing, because the same emotion chemicals are released in the brain! As Glouberman says, 'A good way to think of it is that energy follows thought, what we do follows in the pathway or fits into the thought form created by our imagination. We need to be careful about what we imagine, for we may unknowingly become it' (1989, p50).

Here are some quotations to inspire you, so that you can further inspire children to put flesh on the bones of their dreams, through artistic expression

The poet may speak of 'the music of what might happen, the music of desire, the music of the wonder tales. Let there be a flag flown for spaciousness and pleasure.' (Heaney)

A work of art is abundant, spills out, gets drunk, sits up with you all night and forgets to close the curtains . . . The inexhaustible energy of art is transfusion for a worn-out world. (Winterson, 1995, p65)

People need to begin to allow themselves to conceive of being different from the way they are. Thus a bridge is created between the current reality and the 'conceivable self'. (Clarkson, 1989, p106)

It may be through manipulation of his created elements that he discovers new possibilities of feeling, strange moods, perhaps greater concentrations of passion than his own temperament could ever produce, or than his fortunes have yet called forth. (Langer, 1953, p374)

Yeats believes that, if we are able to focus completely on a thought in an imaginary vision, then this idea will realise itself in the circumstances of life . . . (McNiff, 1992, p223)

CONSIDERING FURTHER COUNSELLING OR THERAPY FOR CHILDREN WHO HAVE DIFFICULTY WISHING, HOPING OR DREAMING FOR THEMSELVES

> Therapy is permission to be exuberant, to have gladness, to play with the nicest possibilities for ourselves within our short lives. (Zinker, 1978, p19)

Even if a very defeated or hopeless child meets with good luck in later life, he may be unable to use it. This is because whatever changes occur in his outer world, he always carries his inner world with him, and with it his deeply ingrained sense of defeat or hopelessness. Something must change in the defeated child's *inner* world before he can start really using, getting excited by or going after dreams in his outer world. Hence the importance for such children of therapeutic intervention and the deep psychological messages of therapeutic story that are received on an inner-world level. Effective child counselling or therapy will enable the troubled child to work in depth with his imagination – with his deepest and most meaningful images. With an effective therapist, children so often begin to speak in very powerful poetry. This is because effective therapy will enrich their capacity to visualise to imagine different worlds, and so to foster hopes and dreams.

For a child who is following someone else's star, it can take counselling or therapy to help him re-establish contact with his real self. This is often a vital precursor to the child knowing what he wants, rather than knowing only about what someone else wants him to want.

Counselling or therapy can help a child who has a crushed will to find the determination and drive that he may have lost in early infancy. In effective child therapy or counselling, the creativity of the therapist comes into play with that of the child, bringing about the richest kind of interaction possible. This provides vital nourishment for the child's own creative imagination. In short, therapy can help the child who has lost hope in there being a supportive, encouraging world, to find it again.

BIBLIOGRAPHY

Berne E, 1964, *Games People Play*, Grove Press, New York.

Clarkson P, 1993, Personal communication.

Clarkson P, 1995, *Gestalt Counselling in Action*, Sage, London.

Davis M & Wallbridge D, 1981, *Boundary and Space: An Introduction to the Work of DW Winnicott*, Karnac/Brunner Mazel, London/New York.

Daws D, 1997, 'The Perils of Intimacy: Closeness and Distance in Feeding and Weaning', *Journal of Child Psychotherapy*, 23(2), pp179-99.

Freud S, 1926, 'Inhibitions, Symptoms and Anxiety', pp. 237-333 in *On Psychopathology, Inhibitions, Symptoms and Anxiety*, Vol 10 of *The Penguin Freud Library* (Richards A & Strachey J eds, Strachey J, trans), Penguin, Harmondsworth.

Gersie A & King N, 1990, *Storymaking in Education and Therapy*, Jessica Kingsley, London.

Glouberman D, 1989, *Life Choices and Life Changes Through Imagework: The Art of Developing Personal Vision*, Unwin Hyman, London.

Glucksman M, 1987, 'Clutching at Straws: An Infant's Response to Lack of Maternal Containment', *British Journal of Psychotherapy*, 3(4), pp347-49.

Jeffers S, 1987, *Feel the Fear and Do it Anyway*, Arrow, London.

Keenan B, 1992, *An Evil Cradling*, Vintage, London.

Khan MM, 1989, *Hidden Selves: Between Theory and Practice*, Maresfield, London.

Langer SK, 1953, *Feeling and Form*, Scribner's, New York.

McNiff S, 1992, *Art As Medicine*, Piatkus, London.

Nietzsche F, 1993, *The Sayings of Friedrich Nietzsche* (ed Martin S), Duckworth, London.

Person ES, 1996, *The Force of Fantasy*, Harper Collins, London.

Rowan J, 1986, *Ordinary Ecstasy: Humanistic Psychology in Action*, Routledge & Kegan Paul, London.

Sunderland M, 1993, *Draw On Your Emotions*, Speechmark Publishing, Bicester.

Sunderland M, 2000, *Using Story Telling as a Therapeutic Tool with Children*, Speechmark Publishing, Bicester.

Thrail E, 1994, *Retrospect: The Story of an Analysis*, Quartet, London.

Winnicott DW, 1949, 'The World in Small Doses', reprinted in Winnicott DW, 1964, *The Child, the Family and the Outside World*, Penguin, London.

Winterson J, 1995, *Art Objects*, Jonathan Cape, London.

Yalom D I, 1980, *Existential Psychotherapy*, Basic Books, New York.

Zinker J, 1978, *Creative Process in Gestalt Therapy*, Vintage, New York.

Helping Children With Feelings
Margot Sunderland, illustrated by Nicky Armstrong

This is a ground-breaking pack of nine beautifully illustrated stories which have been designed to help children who are troubled in their lives. The stories act as vehicles to help children think about and connect with their feelings. Each is accompanied by a guidebook that will prove a vital resource when using the stories. Featured below are details about five of the titles and an accompanying handbook.

Using Story Telling as a Therapeutic Tool with Children

This practical manual begins with the philosophy and psychology underpinning the therapeutic value of story telling. It shows how to use story telling as a therapeutic tool with children and how to make an effective response when a child tells a story to you. It is an essential accompaniment to the series: Helping Children with Feelings. Covers such issues as:

◆ Why story telling is such a good way of helping children with their feelings;

◆ What resources you may need in a story-telling session;

◆ How to construct your own therapeutic story for a child;

◆ What to do when children tell stories to you;

◆ Things to do and things to say when working with a child's story.

Approx 132pp, illustrated, paperback

Willy and the Wobbly House
Helping children who are anxious or obsessional

Willy is an anxious boy who experiences the world as a very unsafe wobbly place where anything awful might happen at any time. Joe, the boy next door, is too ordered and tidy to be able to ever really enjoy life. Willy longs for order while Joe longs for things to wobble. However, when they meet Mrs Flop she tells them they don't have to put up with feeling as they do. At her suggestion they visit the Puddle People who help them break out of their fixed patterns and find far richer ways of living in the world.

Storybook: 32pp, A4, full colour throughout, wire-stitched
Guidebook: 60pp, A4, illustrated, wire-o-bound

The Frog Who Longed for the Moon to Smile
Helping children who yearn for someone they love

Frog is very much in love with the moon because the moon once smiled at him. Now he spends all his time gazing at the moon and dreaming about her. He waits and waits for her to smile at him again. One day a wise and friendly crow helps Frog to see how he is wasting his life away. Eventually Frog takes the huge step of turning away from the moon. When he does, he feels a terrible emptiness and loneliness. He has not yet seen what is on the other side of him. When in time he looks around, he is lit up by everything he sees. All the time he has been facing the place of very little, he's had his back to the place of plenty.

Storybook: 32pp, A4, full colour throughout, wire-stitched
Guidebook: 48pp, A4, illustrated, wire-o-bound

A Nifflenoo Called Nevermind
Helping children who bottle up their feelings

Nevermind always carries on whatever happens! Each time something horrible happens to him he is very brave and simply says 'never mind'. He meets with all kinds of setbacks, bullying and disappointments but each time he just tucks his feelings away and carries on with life. However, he becomes so full of bottled-up feelings that after a time he gets stuck in a hedge. In addition, some of these feelings start to leak out of him in ways that hurt others. Luckily he happens upon a bogwert who helps him understand that his feelings do matter and should not be ignored. Nifflenoo then learns how to both express his feelings and stand up for himself.

Storybook: 36pp, A4, full colour throughout, wire-stitched
Guidebook: 48pp, A4, illustrated, wire-o-bound

A Pea Called Mildred
Helping children pursue their hopes and dreams

Mildred is a pea with dreams. She has great plans for her pea life. However, people are always telling her that her dreams are pointless as she is just another ordinary pea. As she is not prepared to be just another ordinary pea and let go of her dreams, she goes into a very lonely place. Eventually, with the help of a kind person along the way, Mildred ends up doing exactly what she has always dreamed of doing.
Storybook: 28pp, A4, full colour throughout, wire-stitched
Guidebook: 28pp, A4, illustrated, wire-o-bound

A Wibble Called Bipley (and a Few Honks)
Helping children who have hardened their hearts or become bullies

Bipley is a warm cuddly creature, but the trouble is someone has broken his heart. He feels so hurt that he decides it is just too painful to ever love again. When he meets some big tough Honks in the wood, they teach him how to harden his heart so that he doesn't have to feel hurt anymore. Bipley turns into a bully. To begin with he feels powerful but gradually he realises that the world has turned terribly grey. Luckily, Bipley meets some creatures who teach him how he can protect himself without hardening his heart.

Storybook: 44pp, A4, full colour throughout, wire-stitched
Guidebook: 60pp, A4, illustrated, wire-o-bound

Routledge
Taylor & Francis Group
www.routledge.com

2 Park Square, Milton Park, Abingdon, Oxon OX14 4RN